T0198686

You are CLEAN!

KELLY KAINER BILLINGTON

As we go through life from day to day,

we must be clean in every way!

Our body, heart, soul, and mind

should be clean all the time!

You may not know it,
but our body is God's temple!

And taking good care of it
is really important and quite simple!

Always remember, we are what we eat!
Good food choices are hard to beat!

All Natural Foods

We should eat fresh and natural foods
to keep our bodies running smooth!

*Being active and exercising
keeps our body strong and thriving!*

*Building muscles and staying flexible
makes us WINNERS and UNDEFEATABLE!*

A clean home is essential in many ways.

It is where we start and end most of our days!

When you have a messy room,
it can bring a feeling of doom and gloom!

On the other hand, when your room is clean,
it helps to bring happy dreams!

In the morning and
before you say good night,

brushing your teeth
keeps them white and bright!

**Remember that cleanliness
is next to Godliness!**

**So keeping your hands washed and your bodies bathed
is essential to living clean every day**

A clean mind is also quite a blessing!
To keep it clean, here is a lesson:

Good thoughts make a clean mind!
Keep your mind busy with no idle time!

When it comes to a clean heart and soul,
life can be really good I am told!

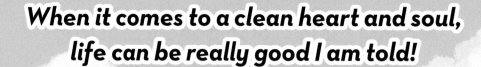

We are LOVED!
And we are FORGIVEN!

When you love and forgive every girl and boy,
your heart and soul simply LEAP for JOY!

So as we go through life from day to day,
and we live clean lives in every way!

Know that God loves you
not just for being clean and for what you do!

**But God loves you
simply because YOU are YOU!**

ABOUT THE AUTHOR

Kelly Kainer Billington is blessed to be a mother of one amazing son and a grandmother (Nana) of two awesome grandsons! And she advocates that her family and God are most important to her.

She earned her Bachelor of Science degree in Business Administration-Management w/Teacher Certification. After 12 years in public schools, she felt a calling to enter the real estate world. She became a broker, investor, renovator, and she continues to manage the family businesses in honor of her beloved husband who went to be with the Lord in 2022.

She authors and creates her own website at www.kellykainerbillington.com. She has included a beautiful tribute to her beloved Mother on her JOY Comes in the Morning web page. She created this page to honor her Mother whose middle name was JOY, and to honor her courageous 12-year battle with Alzheimer's. Kelly has written and copyrighted a documentary in regard to their experiences with the Alzheimer's disease. She has created a link to share this information on her website as well. She knows her Mother would be sporting that infamous MiMi smile if it were to help just one person, which simply reflects the essence of her beautiful Mother!

Kelly has written another children's book titled, God's Goodness in You and Me, which focuses on bringing God back to family life! She is also the author of the up and coming NANA and ME Series! This series focuses on things like the Golden Rule in the book titled, You are GOLDEN!, Honesty is the best Policy in the book titled, You are HONEST!, and Cleanliness is next to Godliness in a book titled, You are CLEAN!, with more to come!

As Kelly continues to move forward in her career as an author, she hopes to help and inspire people of all ages with her publications!

WestBow Press books may be ordered through booksellers or by contacting:

WestBow Press
A Division of Thomas Nelson & Zondervan
1663 Liberty Drive
Bloomington, IN 47403
www.westbowpress.com
844-714-3454

Interior Image Credit: Daniel Majan

Bible Scripture:
New American Bible, New International Version

ISBN: 978-1-6642-6867-8 (sc)
ISBN: 978-1-6642-6868-5 (e)

Library of Congress Control Number: 2022910883

Print information available on the last page.

WestBow Press rev. date: 07/18/2022

WESTBOW
PRESS®
A DIVISION OF THOMAS NELSON
& ZONDERVAN

Printed in the United States
by Baker & Taylor Publisher Services